DATE DUE

2001

DISCARDED

PRINTED IN U.S.A.

EXPLORING
BUSINESS
AND
ECONOMICS

EXPLORING BUSINESS AND ECONOMICS

Taxes

Norman L. Macht

Chelsea House Publishers
Philadelphia

Frontis: **Throughout history, taxation has been used as a means to pay and prepare for war. U.S. tax dollars paid for this F-22 military Raptor jet.**

CHELSEA HOUSE PUBLISHERS

EDITOR-IN-CHIEF Sally Cheney
DIRECTOR OF PRODUCTION Kim Shinners
PRODUCTION MANAGER Pamela Loos
ART DIRECTOR Sara Davis

Choptank Syndicate/Chestnut Productions

EDITORIAL Norman Macht and Mary Hull
PRODUCTION Lisa Hochstein
PICTURE RESEARCH Norman Macht

http://www.chelseahouse.com

First Printing

1 3 5 7 9 8 6 4 2

Library of Congress Cataloging-in-Publication Data

Macht, Norman L. (Norman Lee), 1929–
    Taxes / Norman Macht.
    p. cm. — (Exploring business and economics)
    ISBN 0-7910-6640-1 (alk. paper)
1. Taxation. 2. Income tax. I. Title. II. Series.
HJ2305.M255 2001
336.2—dc21   2001042509

Table of Contents

Members of the Massachusetts Council of Minutemen and Militia toss over tea from crates aboard the brig *Beaver* into Boston Harbor on December 14, 1997, in Boston for the 224th anniversary reenactment of the Boston Tea Party. The Boston Tea Party is one of the most famous tax revolts of all time.

The Boston Tea Party

An icy winter wind blew through the streets of Boston on Thursday evening, December 16, 1773, at 6 P.M. The last pale pink remnants of sunset had long since faded into darkness. A thin sliver of moon cast no light on a group of more than 100 men and boys, ranging in age from 14 to 45, some of them whooping and hollering as they marched in disorganized ranks toward the nearby docks.

To cloak their identity, most of them had smeared their faces with red clay, soot, burnt cork, or lampblack, and covered their heads with old blankets, shawls, dresses, or rags. Some tried to look and act like war-dancing Indians.

Their destination was three ships tied up at Griffin's wharf. Their target was 342 chests filled with tea.

The commotion attracted hundreds of people who were just leaving a noisy meeting at Old South Church concerning the same subject: tea. None of them was protesting against tea, a beverage as popular among Americans at that time as coffee is today. The object of their outrage was **taxes.**

The colonists were not against all taxes. They realized that their local governments needed money to pay for building and lighting the cobblestone streets in the cities, operating local councils and courts, providing water supplies, and other community needs. They were willing to pay the taxes approved by their elected House of Representatives.

Although they considered themselves loyal Englishmen, they objected to taxes being imposed on them by the Parliament in faraway London, where they had no voice and no elected representatives. Their protests against taxation without representation had begun 10 years earlier.

Death and Taxes

The spirit of the colonists' protests against British taxes was reflected in the songs and slogans of the Revolutionary War. One tavern song began:

"Rally Mohawks! Bring out your axes,
And tell King George we'll pay no taxes."

Banners bore the words "Taxation without representation is tyranny!"

The ever-wise Ben Franklin recognized the inevitability of some things when he wrote, "Nothing is certain in life except death and taxes."

Dressed as a patriotic citizen of Boston, c. 1773, a costumed man throws a crate of tea into Boston Harbor during a reenactment of the Boston Tea Party, in which New Englanders protested England's import duty on tea, one of the most popular beverages in the colonies.

Prior to 1763 they had never been tapped for **revenue** by the British government. When King George III and his Parliament decided that the colonies should foot the bill for maintaining the army of 10,000 British soldiers stationed among them, the Americans objected. They didn't want all those redcoats camped in their cities and towns to defend them against nonexistent enemies in the first place, and they certainly weren't about to pay for them through any British taxes.

By means of **smuggling,** harassing tax collectors, or refusing to buy any goods imported from England, the colonists had sabotaged British efforts to tax them since

1763. This latest attempt, thinly disguised as a **duty,** was a tax on tea, coupled with a law prohibiting the colonies from importing tea from anywhere else but Britain. Parliament was determined to prove that they had the power to tax the Americans. The colonists were equally determined to deny them that right.

Three ships, the *Dartmouth, Eleanor,* and *Beaver,* carrying tea and other cargo, had arrived in Boston harbor in late November and early December. The duty had to be paid when the tea was unloaded. The expense would be passed on to the people buying the tea. The leaders of the protest had tried to persuade the ships' owners to send the ships back to England with the tea still in their holds. The owners either refused or were prevented from doing so by the king's appointed governor. All the talks and angry meetings and rallies had failed to resolve the stalemate. Now, anticipating the imminent unloading of the tea, it was time for action.

The mob was orderly as they reached the three ships. They had no intention of causing any harm to the ships, their other cargoes, or the few crew members and guards. Armed with axes, they boarded the ships and, meeting no resistance, began the job they had come to do.

It was hard work. A full tea chest weighed more than 300 pounds. Each one had to be hauled to a position beneath an opening in the deck where rope and tackle were attached to hoist it up on deck. There the wooden chests were hacked open, the tea dumped over the side, followed by the splintered pieces of the chests.

Lit by lanterns and torches, the work went slowly and steadily. The original group was augmented by more volunteers who came out of the crowd, which stood shrouded in an eerie silence, broken only by the sounds of cracking wood and splashing jetsam. It was low tide; the ships rested on the bottom in two feet of water. The mountains of dumped tea and broken crates rose higher than the decks.

It took three hours for the last of the chests to be jettisoned, the last flurries of loose tea leaves to be swept from the decks and stray leaves shaken from shoes. As tempting as it was to scoop up some free tea and carry it home, nobody did. (One man found some shredded leaves in his shoes when he returned home. He put them in a little bottle and saved them. The bottle is believed to be still in the family's possession.) The task completed, with no damage to any other property and only one raider injured in an accident, the people quietly made their way home.

Before the night was over, Paul Revere was on his horse riding to New York with news of the Boston Tea Party. The word quickly spread, uniting the colonies. Ships carrying tea to other ports were turned away and ordered to carry their cargoes back to London. In some cities colonists built bonfires of tea leaves as a symbol of their support for the Bostonians.

Three months later Parliament ordered Boston Harbor closed to all shipping until the people paid for the destroyed tea. The Massachusetts colonists refused to pay. In April 1774 the British sent more troops to keep order. One year later the first shot was fired in the Revolutionary War, sparked by a protest over taxes.

In ancient times taxes might be paid in crops, livestock, or even labor. Some historians believe the workers who built the pyramids may have been paying a tax to the Egyptian government in the form of their labor.

The First Taxes

Taxes are as old as civilization, and taxpayers' dislike of them goes back just as far. More than 5,000 years ago, a region known as Mesopotamia, where Iraq is today, was settled by tribes that came out of the mountains of what are now Turkey and Iran. These settlements gradually grew into cities, each one independent of the others, a city-state unto itself.

As the settlements grew, the region became known as Sumer, and the individual city-states had names like Ur, Lagash, and Umma. Most of the people in this hot, dry climate were farmers. They grew grains, vegetables, and date palms, and raised livestock, such as cattle, sheep, and goats. Others were artisans, making objects from stone, gold, silver, copper, and cloth. A few were traders.

At the top of the social scale stood the priests of the temples; the slaves were at the bottom. The majority of the people were free to own houses and farms, and to sell the products of their labor. They could work hard in pursuit of wealth, or work just enough to get by.

Systems of laws, government, religion, and business began to evolve. Money was based on the weight of a lump of gold or silver. A mina weighed about one pound; a shekel equaled one-sixtieth of a mina.

Although the land of Sumer was ruled by a king, most of the power resided in the rulers of the cities. It is in the nature of the powerful to seek still more power, and the ancient Sumerians were no different. Rulers of the stronger states cast greedy eyes on the weaker ones. They formed armies, equipped them with swords and armor, and sent them out to conquer their neighbors.

All that took money. They got it by creating a variety of schemes to demand payments from the people: farmers and merchants, traders and fishermen, rich and poor. Nobody escaped the tax collectors.

The early tax codes were simple and easy to enforce. Tax collectors went everywhere, traveling from farm to farm, counting the lambs or cattle or harvested grain, and taking some or most or all of it. From boatmen they took the boats. When a shepherd brought a sheep to the shearing shop, the tax collector was there to take five shekels from him. The mixer of perfumed oils paid a tax when he sold his wares. If a man divorced a woman, he paid a tax. When someone died, the family paid a tax on the burial. If they had no shekels, then grain, bread, or beer might be accepted instead.

The rulers found the system to be so profitable, the tax collections continued when the wars ended. "There's nothing so permanent as a temporary tax," may be the oldest joke in the world.

The city-state of Lagash enjoyed the first tax reduction in history when a new, reform-minded ruler, Urukagina, cut or eliminated most of the taxes. No longer were tax collectors seen throughout the land. But the reformer didn't last long. Lagash became so poor and defenseless, a more powerful state, Umma, conquered them.

From the time of King David in 1000 B.C., the kingdoms of Israel, Assyria, Babylon, and Persia all used some form of taxation to support armies and erect public buildings. Payments might be made in grain from the fields, fruit from the orchards, or even the sweat of a man's brow; a tax could be paid in labor, from stone cutting to manning the oars in a warship.

The city-state of Athens was in the early stages of a form of democracy in the sixth century B.C. Before that experi-

Taxing the Poor

Roman subjects could be taxed even if they owned nothing. The Roman historian Livy told the story of a soldier who, while away fighting in a war, "had not only lost his year's crop after the destruction of his farm, but also his cottage had been burned down, all his possessions stolen, and his flocks driven off; on top of that, taxes were levied during those hard times, forcing him to borrow money."

Unable to pay the interest on the debt, the soldier could have been executed or sold into slavery to settle the debt. He was spared and taken to the workhouse instead.

Workers pick tea leaves at a plantation in central China's Hunan province in 2001. At one time tea in China was so heavily taxed, the tea industry almost disappeared.

ment got very far, a tyrant gained control with the support of the peasants. He promised to give them the money to purchase farm equipment. He gave them jobs building roads and temples and other public works. To pay for all that, he raised the money by taxing the wealthy, taking part of their crops. This was an early example of a politician rising to power by promising to transfer money from one group to another through taxes.

About 100 years later Athens reached the height of its prosperity and glory. There were no direct taxes on income. Most of the public parks and buildings were constructed by wealthy citizens, who also provided entertainments and other public services. This made them popular in the community. Every rich man tried to do more for the people to top his wealthy friends. Everyone enjoyed the benefits. No taxes were needed.

That changed, as usual, when there was a war. Then taxes on property became necessary to pay for the armies. A war that lasted 27 years between Athens and Sparta cost a lot of money for both sides.

The people of the conquered lands were fair game to be looted by heavy taxes. Their treasure was carried back to the victors' palaces, or used to pay the costs of the occupying armies.

The Greek conquerors depended on the wealthy elite of the occupied city-states to collect the taxes for them. At the same time, wealthy citizens provided public facilities and entertainments out of their own pockets to keep the population contented. Farmers paid taxes by giving a share of their crops to the city-state. Artisans and merchants paid according to their trade: from bakers to barbers to mummy embalmers, collectors charged what they thought each trade was worth, regardless of how good or bad business was. Tanners used human urine in the curing of leather. When they made their rounds of the public bathrooms, they paid a tax on what they collected.

Penalties for nonpayment of taxes were harsh. These were not citizens taxing themselves for community needs, but foreign occupiers with no local ties or interest in the welfare of the conquered people. When Egypt was under Greek rule, if a man was late paying his taxes, the collectors could beat him, laying on one stroke for each day he was late. Tax cheaters might have their nose or an ear cut off.

The Golden Age of Athens did not last long. When the Macedonians, then Alexander the Great, and later the Romans conquered Greece, the heavy hand of the invaders' tax collectors fell upon them.

The Romans were fierce tax collectors. They devised so many ways to take goods and money from the people they ruled, they had to create an entire bureaucracy of record keepers to keep track of it all. That wasn't easy; the Arabic numerals we use today would not exist for another 1,000 years. It was difficult to keep accurate records without them.

There were other problems. The Roman Empire extended over thousands of square miles. It ruled different cultures from Britain and Spain in the west, all the way around the Mediterranean to Egypt and Israel. There was no way they could maintain an efficient tax collecting system. There were no highways. It took weeks for money or messages to be carried from the outlying provinces to Rome.

They decided it would be easier for them to collect the taxes by selling the collection rights to a businessman called a **publican.** In this way, the government received its money for the year immediately. It was then up to the publican to go out and collect it as best he could from the people in the province he had paid for. In order to show a profit, he had to collect more than he had paid for the rights. The more he could squeeze out of the people, the higher his profit would be.

Backed by the law and the Roman army, publicans extracted money from the powerless peasants. The collectors were not above employing a little torture if they thought a peasant was hiding a flock of sheep. If a farmer or merchant had no money or property to pay the taxes, the publican would lend it to them at high **interest.** Sometimes families had to sell their children to pay their debts.

In ancient times tax collectors took part of a farmer's crop. But property taxes in America have to be paid in cash. When a farmer has no money to pay his taxes, the farm and equipment or livestock may be sold at auction to pay the taxes.

No wonder the publicans, and the local residents they employed as collectors, were hated in every corner of the far-flung empire. Whenever publicans or tax collectors are mentioned in the Bible, it is never complimentary. The Sermon on the Mount refers to publicans, casting them among the lowest forms of life. The people resented having Roman soldiers in their midst. They resented paying taxes that went into faraway Roman palaces. But they reserved their deepest hatred for their neighbors who collected the taxes for their enemies.

This Roman 22 carat gold coin dates from the time of Roman rule in Britain. The Romans invented new ways of collecting both goods and money as taxes.

This system lasted for a hundred years. Then civil servants were employed to collect the taxes, replacing the publicans.

Times were not always cruel for the taxpayers in the provinces ruled by Rome. Some emperors reduced taxes, or waived them when a region was struck by a devastating drought or earthquake.

In Judea the Romans taxed the crops but demanded that the tax be paid in money. There was also an annual head tax of one denarius (equal to an average day's wages) on all men age 14 to 65 and women age 12 and older. Property taxes were also levied.

On top of the Roman taxes, cities had their own set of taxes to pay for community services and buildings. These high taxes caused many farmers to move away from the empire's lands during its declining years in the fourth century. To prevent them from leaving, the Romans passed laws that allowed landlords to shackle the peasants who worked their land. The children were legally bound to do the same work as their fathers.

In China, taxes on land and agriculture provided most of the rulers' revenues until the eighth century, when the growing and drinking of tea became a big business. There was a 10 percent tax on tea, bamboo, wood, lacquer, silk, straw, and cash. As the tea trade grew, a complex web of taxes and regulations became so heavy it almost destroyed the industry.

During the Middle Ages, taxes were assessed on communities and villages rather than individuals. Thus, when the king and his party came to a castle for a visit, people in the area might be ordered to supply so much money, bread, and meat to feed the royal party.

Feudal lords depended on the peasants to do all the work, produce the crops, and pay taxes, too. The Pope taxed the churches, the kings taxed the barons, and everybody taxed the peasants. General property taxes were the main source of revenue for the next few hundred years. Of course, when there were wars—and there were many wars—anyone and anything might be taken by the tax collectors.

A taxpayer tries to determine which of over 80 different tax forms she may need to file her income taxes with the Internal Revenue Service. Filing a tax return has become so complicated that the average person is unable to do it without professional help.

The Income Tax

The federal **income tax,** which today provides about half the United States government's revenue and touches the lives of almost every American, did not become a permanent part of American life until 100 years after the Revolutionary War. But it was not a new idea.

Primitive types of income taxes were used more than 2,000 years ago in India and Asia. They involved a lot of guessing, since very few merchants and traders kept any kind of records. In 1189 A.D. the kings of England and France imposed an income tax to finance the Third Crusade, a military expedition by Christians to try to recapture Jerusalem from the Muslims.

In the late 15th century and again during the Napoleonic wars around 1800, Britain added an income tax to its property taxes to pay the soaring costs of armies and navies at war. When the war ended, the income tax ended, only to be revived in 1842, when it became permanent.

Florence, Italy, a powerful independent city-state during the Renaissance (1200–1700 A.D.), introduced a graduated income tax: higher incomes were taxed at higher rates, reaching a maximum of 50 percent. (A 50 percent tax rate doesn't mean that you pay half your income; it means that earnings above a certain amount are taxed at that rate.)

In the American colonies, taxes varied from one region to another. Prior to independence, there was little local government and few public buildings. Many of the roads were privately built and maintained, the owners collecting the tolls. The most widely used form of taxation was on land holdings, except in the south, which relied more on duties paid on **imports** and **exports.**

The head tax—so much per adult male—and **excise,** or sales, taxes on items such as wine, carriages, coffee, and tea, were common. An excise tax was paid by the merchant or trader; the consumer paid the **sales tax.** Of course, in the end, the consumer paid all the taxes, as they were built into the price.

In New England the old Greek method of estimated income taxes was used; they called it a **faculty tax.** It was based on a man's trade, not his income. A blacksmith or printer, for example, paid so much, regardless of his income.

The British attempt to impose taxes on the colonies ignited the Revolutionary War and led to American independence. But with freedom came responsibilities. The Continental Congress had no power to tax anybody. They

There was a time when taxes on whiskey and tobacco brought in enough revenue to pay most of the cost of the United States government. Today tobacco is heavily taxed to discourage people from smoking.

had to beg and borrow and invent their own kind of money to finance the fighting of the war. Soldiers went unpaid, unfed, poorly clothed. But they won anyhow.

The ink had barely dried on the peace treaty of 1783 before the first American tax revolt erupted over property taxes in Massachusetts. The separate states were reluctant to give the central government any taxing powers. They had had enough of kings and tyrants with too much power. The writers of the Constitution debated this issue for several years. Finally they concluded that the country could not defend itself and carry out the responsibilities of a real nation without the authority to raise the required revenue.

The Constitution, ratified in 1788, gave Congress limited power to tax, prohibiting direct taxation of individuals.

The young republic relied on income derived from excise taxes on such items as sugar, tobacco, slaves, and whiskey; fees for legal documents; and licenses to practice law or sell alcoholic beverages. That led to the second American tax revolt.

Many farmers turned their corn or rye into whiskey. It was easier and more profitable to turn the grain into whiskey, put it in jugs and barrels, and carry them to markets. The farmers resented government agents, called **revenuers,** snooping around their homes and farms looking for illegal whiskey-making equipment called "stills." These revenuers reminded the farmers of the heavy-handed British troops they had fought to be rid of, and they appealed to their Congressmen for relief. Congress hastily

Shays' Rebellion

American citizens usually protest taxes peacefully, voting to limit property taxes, for example. But not all tax protests have been silent.

In 1786 Massachusetts farmers and small property owners rebelled against high property taxes. Led by several men, including one named Daniel Shays, about 600 armed men marched on the courthouse in Springfield. Many of them faced debtors' prison because they didn't have any money to pay their taxes. They hoped to persuade the court to prevent the loss of their farms and freedom. It took the state militia to restore order. Shays escaped to Vermont to avoid being hanged, but he was later pardoned for leading what became known as Shays' Rebellion.

changed the laws so they did not apply to the smaller whiskey makers, or distillers.

That wasn't good enough for the larger farmers of western Pennsylvania. They still refused to pay the whiskey tax, and warned the government agents to stay off their property. A shooting war between federal marshals and the rebels broke out, forcing President George Washington to call on federal troops to put down what became known as the Whiskey Rebellion.

As had been true for thousands of years, wars led to increased taxes. Threats to the new nation from France in 1797–98 and England in the War of 1812 brought about direct taxes on homes, land, and slaves, and the first death or **estate taxes.** An extra tax on imported rum aimed at cutting down consumption was the first instance of using taxes to try to influence social behavior. When the British marched into Washington, D.C., and burned the White House and Capitol in 1814, the outlook was grim for the nation's survival. The first suggestion of a federal income tax was put before Congress. They didn't want to pass such a tax. The war ended before they had to act on it.

For the next 50 years the United States was virtually free of federal taxes. The sale of public lands, primarily in the newly settled west, and duties on imports brought in enough revenue to keep the government wheels turning.

The Civil War changed all that. Even before the first shot was fired on Fort Sumter on April 12, 1861, the government was out of money and in debt. Congress slapped taxes on just about everything that people owned, from feather pillows to pianos. And they passed the nation's first income tax.

Originally a flat rate—three percent on all income over $800 a year—it was changed to a graduated tax (higher

To avoid taxes on whiskey, farmers built illegal alcohol-making equipment called stills, and hid them. Revenue agents have been searching out illegal stills since George Washington was president.

rates on higher incomes) before it went into effect. The law also called for the income reported by people to be published in the newspapers.

The income tax caused a lot of arguments from the day it was passed. Western states, where people owned large spreads of land, but had little cash income, liked the idea of an income tax. The richer, more populous states of the north didn't like it. Many people thought it was illegal. They debated the merits of a **flat tax** versus a graduated scale. Other questions were debated: What **deductions** were fair? What should the maximum rate be? The answers changed from year to year. These same questions are still being debated today.

Now that the income tax existed, Congress had to find a way to collect it. Thus was born the **Internal Revenue Service (IRS),** which was then and remains today the most disliked of all government agencies.

The southern states that had seceded from the union were, of course, not affected by the new tax, but the northern and western states were suddenly flooded with revenue collectors. They worked on a commission basis, which meant that, like the hated publicans of ancient Rome, the more they collected, the more they earned. They went door to door, distributing a tax form to be filled out. People were asked to declare their income for the year, and all their personal belongings. A family that earned too little to be taxed, but owned a piano, might have to pay two dollars on the piano. A few days later the collector returned and picked up the forms and whatever money the family owed.

In 1864 President Abraham Lincoln made so many mistakes on his income tax return, he paid $1,250 more than he had to. It took eight years for his estate to get a refund.

Nobody lost an ear or a nose if they lied about their income or possessions—and people did tend to understate these things—but if the revenuer saw suspicious signs of more wealth than a man was declaring, he could raise the amount of declared income on his own and add a stiff fine to the tax bill.

The Civil War ended, but the income tax continued. Scheduled to end in 1870, it was bringing in so much money, the government kept it going for two more years.

The question remained as to whether the income tax was a direct tax on people as forbidden by the Constitution. In 1880 the Supreme Court ruled that it was not. Fifteen years later, when Congress tried to start it again, the Court decided that it was a direct tax and therefore unconstitutional.

With the costs of the war behind them, the government could live without an income tax, which had provided one quarter of its revenue at one point. It now relied almost entirely on duties on imports, and taxes on liquor and tobacco. The revenuers kept their jobs, but they were now assigned to raiding illegal distilleries making untaxed "moonshine," or whiskey, mostly in the woods and hollows of the southern mountains.

Taxing liquor and tobacco at that time was not done to discourage their use. On the contrary, their widespread consumption guaranteed that these geese would lay a steady production of golden tax eggs. They still do today.

The income tax debate continued for the next 40 years. The **Democrats** generally considered it a fair way to spread the costs of government. The **Republicans** preferred high **tariffs,** which also protected American farmers and manufacturers by imposing higher prices on imported goods. But this made things more expensive for the average person.

Once again war influenced taxes more than politics. The Spanish-American War in 1898 forced Congress to slap taxes on just about every activity and product that people paid for from chewing gum to circuses. Taxes on beer and tobacco doubled; nobody cut down on the use of either.

Other military actions made it necessary to juggle the tax laws every year. It became clear that the government needed a steady, reliable source of revenue: a permanent income tax.

To avoid another court fight, Congress proposed a Constitutional amendment authorizing an income tax. This required approval by at least 36 states. On February 13, 1913, Wyoming became the 36th state to ratify the 16th amendment, which gives Congress the power to collect taxes on incomes.

The tax form 1040—the same one used today—consisted of three pages. On the first you listed your income, deductions, and the amount of tax you owed. On page two you showed where your income came from. On page three you had six deductions you could take. Four of them applied to businesses more than individuals. The other two were interest paid on debts and all other national, state, and local taxes paid.

The top rate was 6 percent, and you had to be very wealthy to pay that much. The first $3,000 of income ($4,000 for married couples) was exempt (free) from the tax. A typical factory worker earned about $500 a year, so few people

Taxes: A Laughing Matter?

The public's dislike of taxes has been a fertile source of humor for centuries. A few examples:

"The art of taxation consists in so plucking the goose as to obtain the largest possible amount of feathers with the smallest possible amount of hissing."

– Jean Baptiste Colber
17th century French statesman

"The income tax has made more liars out of the American people than golf has."

– Will Rogers, 1924
American comedian

"There is one difference between a tax collector and a taxidermist—the taxidermist leaves the hide."

– Mortimer Caplan
former IRS Commissioner

The Union gunboat *Cairo,* shown in this Civil-War era photo, was sunk by Confederates on December 12, 1862, near Vicksburg, Mississippi. Outfitting armies and navies is an expensive business, and the Civil War cost the country so much money, new taxes had to be levied to pay for it all.

paid any tax at all. The first year 357,598 tax returns were filed with the IRS. (In 2000, about 120 million were filed.)

That was it. If your taxes had been withheld by your employer, you might have a refund coming. If you paid too little, there were fines—called penalties—to pay. (One taxpayer who was ordered to pay an additional $2,500 in penalties was so angry he brought a truckload of 250,000 pennies to the IRS office to pay the fine.)

Since that time, through two world wars and other military operations, the income tax has undergone many changes. As social and economic conditions changed, tax rates have been raised and lowered, deductions expanded and reduced, and special **exemptions** added to encourage or discourage people's behavior and influence financial decisions. Every time Congress passes a law to make the income tax fairer or easier to figure out how much you owe, the tax forms have become more complicated. There are now thousands of people who earn their living as tax lawyers and experts in filling out the paperwork for taxpayers.

The original income tax code passed in 1913 was 14 pages long. The Internal Revenue Code of January 2000 was 9,399 pages thick and weighed as much as a roasting chicken. It takes the Treasury Department another 20,000 pages and eight million words of regulations to administer the laws.

The American income tax laws are so long and complicated, nobody really knows what they say, or what the words mean. That's why most people don't even try to fill out the forms themselves. They take all their financial records to an accountant or a tax preparer and pay them to do the work. That's still no guarantee that the forms will be filled out correctly. Six different tax preparers may come up with six different amounts that the taxpayer owes. (Since taxes are taken out of paychecks in advance during the year, some people will get a refund because too much had been taken out.)

What makes it all so difficult? One reason for the confusion is what are called deductions. A deduction is a cost that can be subtracted from your income before you figure out how much is owed. For example, if your parents have borrowed money to buy a house, the interest payments on the mortgage can be deducted from their taxable income. People who wear a uniform in their work, such as policemen, airline crews, and nurses, can deduct the cost of the uniforms. The cost of a business suit cannot be deducted. Actresses and singers and musicians can deduct the cost of their costumes. The cost of traveling for business is deductible, but not for commuting between your home and where you work. Most medical expenses are deductible, as are contributions to charities.

The confusion begins with things that are not so clear: dancing lessons for someone recovering from a broken leg, for instance, or business travel that also includes a vacation at a resort. Should a waiter be taxed on the value of meals he eats in the restaurant where he works? Should a working mother be allowed to deduct what it would cost for a babysitter if Grandma does the sitting? That's why there are special tax courts to hear arguments and settle them. That's why there are thousands of lawyers who specialize in tax cases.

Businesses also pay income taxes. Big corporations have entire staffs to deal with them. Small businesses usually rely on an accountant to take care of their bookkeeping and tax returns.

Income taxes are a hot issue in every presidential election. When the economy is strong and there is little unemployment, it's thought that raising taxes will help to slow things down by taking money out of consumers' hands. If the economy is slowing, cutting taxes will leave people with more money to spend. Some people are always for reducing taxes; others claim that the government needs the money to pay for everything they want it to do. Taxes will always be part of the political debate, because nothing else touches so many lives directly.

Every year Congress talks about making the tax laws simpler and easier to understand. But every time they try to fix them, the laws just get fatter and denser. Some people favor abolishing the income tax altogether and replacing it with a national sales tax. Others would like to throw away the thousands of pages of income tax rules and regulations and replace them with something as simple as: "How much income did you earn last year? Subtract $10,000. Send in 10 percent of what's left."

Such changes are unlikely. The income tax has become a permanent part of American life. The April 15 deadline for sending the tax forms to the Internal Revenue Service remains the most dreaded day on the calendar for many people. About 120 million face the chore of collecting their records for the past year and confronting the forms, or taking it all to the professional tax preparer. The 1040 "Easy" form alone comes with 33 pages of instructions. Many people wait until the last minute, and post offices stay open until midnight that night. Then everybody hopes they didn't make any mistakes, so the IRS will leave them alone for another year.

Space Shuttle Endeavor launches from the Kennedy Space Center. American tax dollars help fund expensive federal projects like the space program.

Where the Money Goes

The United States government collects and spends about two trillion dollars—$2,000,000,000,000—every year. Sometimes they take in a little more than they spend, which is called a **surplus;** sometimes they spend more than they collect, and this is called a **deficit.** Governments don't produce or sell any products. Virtually all the money they spend comes from taxes paid by individuals and businesses.

How they spend the money is called a **budget,** which must be approved by Congress each year. The Constitution gives Congress the power to create and collect taxes. The only thing it says about how to spend the money is "to pay the debts and

Building dams to control rivers, prevent flooding, and generate hydro-electric power is one use of federal tax money. Shown is the Shasta Dam in California with Mt. Shasta in the background.

provide for the common defense and general welfare of the United States."

The Constitution was written soon after the Revolutionary War had been won. Paying the debts came first. The new nation began in debt, having borrowed money to keep the Continental Army going. Repaying those people who had helped them in a time of need, and maintaining a good credit rating were important to the country's leaders.

The United States was a small, weak, newborn nation surrounded by former and possible future enemies. They had no regular army or navy. The English still owned Canada, and their army perched on America's northern border. The French had helped the colonials win the war, but only because the English were their enemies. Much of the land west of the Mississippi River belonged to Spain, and would soon come under French control. The writers of the Constitution knew that individual state militias could not defend the entire nation. So the need to protect and defend their country was a top priority for spending whatever tax revenues they could raise.

It's the "general welfare" language in the Constitution that has led to thousands of government programs, and it is what causes the most heated arguments every year in Congress. "General welfare" can cover anything, from exploring outer space to studying how Frisbies fly.

Protests over taxes—how they are collected and how the money is spent—are as old as taxes themselves. It is in the nature of the tax collector's job to ask questions, pry into people's business, and doubt the truth of what he is told. In 1875 the head of the IRS agreed that the work of the tax collector led "to inquiries into people's affairs, the condition of their business, their losses and gains, matters which most people prefer keeping secret.'"

Just as the tax collectors were hated in the Roman Empire, IRS agents have been threatened with shotguns, dynamite, and pistols. There is probably no more unpopular job a person can have.

Some antitax activists continue to fight the legality of the income tax, claiming it is unconstitutional, illegal, un-American, unfair—and that if it isn't, it ought to be. Every such argument has lost in the courts. Despite their efforts, the income tax is still with us.

By far the most widespread protests have to do with how the tax revenue is spent. And the cause of most of those protests is the same as the cause of much of the taxation throughout history: wars. Since ancient times, there have always been parts of any population that were against whatever the war was at the time.

In America, protests against taxes began as far back as the 1600s. Some religious groups opposed any form of military spending. The writer Henry David Thoreau spent a day in jail for refusing to pay a tax, as a way of objecting to the United States role in the Mexican War from 1846 to 1848. Some people objected to the use of their taxes for military spending during World War I and II.

Pork Barrel Spending

The spending of taxpayers' money on congressmen's pet projects in their home districts or states—projects that have little or no national benefits—is called pork. The term comes from the 19th century practice of curing salt pork in barrels and dipping into the barrels to feed the slaves in the fields. Laws passed to spend money in this way are called pork-barrel laws.

Most of the pork goes to build highways to nowhere in scantily populated areas, and waterways that nobody asked for or will get much use from. Example: $3 billion to dig a duplicate of the Mississippi River running from Mississippi to the Gulf of Mexico.

Other projects of the 1990s included a $500,000 museum in the North Dakota birthplace of television bandleader Lawrence Welk, a model of the Great Wall of China in southern Indiana, and $15 million to plant trees in Iowa.

Studies are another favorite use of the pork barrel. Studies financed by taxpayers have dealt with cow flatulence, the danger of being hit by pieces of old space satellites falling from the sky in New Mexico, jet lag, the time needed to cook eggs, the possibility of generating electricity from the Northern Lights, why people are rude, and why they fall in love.

Demonstrations against military spending reached their height during America's most unpopular war, the Vietnam War in the 1960s. Thousands of people showed up for protest rallies. Internal Revenue offices were picketed. Some protestors paid only half of the taxes they owed, refusing to pay the half that went toward the war expenses in the national budget.

None of these protests have prevented the government from collecting what is owed. The IRS can and does seize property belonging to people who fail to pay their taxes. The IRS then sells the property to collect what it is owed.

Two women in particular fought long battles against taxation and both lost their personal tax wars. One, a corporation president named Vivian Kellems, fought over her tax bill for more than 20 years and never won a battle. Another, Irene Whetstone, an industrial engineer, even spent some time in jail. She claimed that her tax dollars would be spent on illegal projects.

One group did defeat the IRS, although it took four years for them to achieve this victory. The battle ground was not the income tax, but the **Social Security** tax. Social Security is a government pension plan for retired and disabled workers. Its opponents were a religious group, the Amish, many of whom live in Pennsylvania.

The Amish did not believe in insurance, and they considered Social Security to be a form of social insurance. They refused to pay the tax. The IRS said they had to pay. The Amish dug in their heels and said no. The IRS began taking the property of the Amish farmers. They seized their bank accounts.

One spring day an Amish farmer, Valentine Y. Byler, was plowing his field behind a pair of horses. The Amish do not use modern machinery. Three IRS agents went into the field, stopped Byler, took the horses, the harness, and the plow, and left Byler standing in the middle of his field. Later they auctioned off his belongings to pay his Social Security taxes. But four years later, Congress passed a law exempting the Amish from paying the tax.

Many taxpayers get upset when they think the government is wasting their money. The publicity given to the occasional screwdriver that shows up in the records of the Defense Department as costing $500, or congressmen's trips, called junkets, to study conditions in sunny South Seas or Caribbean islands in the middle of winter, stirs up taxpayers' anger. It doesn't bother them enough for them to refuse to pay their taxes. But such incidents raise the level of resistance to further tax increases.

Once in a while even a Congressman will complain about waste. A senator from Wisconsin, William Proxmire, used to give out annual awards for the most outrageous ways taxpayers were fleeced (had their money taken away for a poor or phony reason). Some of the winners included studies on how Frisbies fly and why monkeys clench their jaws.

Agencies are created and never seem to die, even when they have no purpose. One, the Federal Metal and Nonmetallic Mine Safety Board of Review, was created in 1970. The man in charge of the office showed up for work every day for five years, and never had anything to do. No cases were ever sent to him to review. Finally he got tired of drinking coffee and looking out the window all day. He recommended that Congress abolish his job. His unusual request got a lot of publicity from the media before Congress agreed to stop paying for the empty office.

Unlike a simple household budget, the federal budget is so complex that a roomful of accountants would be unable to agree on whether the government was spending more or

Department of Revenue workers process state income tax returns. Only nine U.S. states did not have an income tax as of 2001; residents of the other 41 states must pay both state and federal income tax each year.

less than it was receiving. But, in broad terms, the total pie can be sliced into a few principal pieces. Let's look at where the nation's money goes.

INTEREST ON THE NATIONAL DEBT (12 percent)

The United States was in debt even before it was the United States. The Continental Congress borrowed $11 million from France and Holland and sold war bonds to wealthy supporters in the colonies to fight the Revolutionary War.

In the next 225 years, the debt has grown to almost $6 trillion, a number too large to comprehend. (For only two years, 1834–35, the nation was almost free of debt.) Imagine that much money in this way: if it was all in silver dollars placed side by side, they would circle the equator 6,000 times.

Six times in the nation's history, money was borrowed to pay for wars, causing the biggest increases in the national debt. But in the last 10 years, even with no major wars to pay for, the total debt has almost doubled. In 1916 John D. Rockefeller, the richest man in America, could have paid off the entire national debt out of his own pocket. Today, the two richest men in America couldn't even pay two months' interest on the debt.

Which leads us back to where the money goes. When your parents use a credit card or take out a loan, they have to pay interest—a fee for the use of someone else's money. When the federal government borrows money, they have to pay interest, too. The more they owe, the more interest they have to pay. And if interest rates go up, the cost of borrowing money goes up. That's why 12 cents of every dollar the federal government takes in has to go to pay the interest on the debt, before anything else.

NATIONAL DEFENSE (18 percent)

Nobody questions the need for an adequate military force to protect the country in today's world. The United States stands alone as the most powerful, productive country in the world. Along with that position comes some responsibility for trying to preserve peace as much as possible. But disagreements arise over the missions our armed forces should be used for, how much to pay our soldiers and sailors and flyers, and the kinds of weapons they need to do their job.

American embassies are maintained in many countries to foster cooperation with their governments and assist American travelers and businesses. Economic agencies also work to increase trade and development abroad. Maintaining our military and diplomatic presence in the world takes about 18 cents of every dollar in the national budget.

SOCIAL PROGRAMS (17 percent)

These programs are intended to help provide basic necessities to poor people through food stamps, low-cost public housing, health care, cash supplements, and tax credits. The government spends money on research to find cures for diseases and social service agencies to counsel people who have problems they cannot deal with alone. These programs take 17 cents of every dollar.

PHYSICAL, HUMAN, AND COMMUNITY DEVELOPMENT (9 percent)

This category contains all sorts of things that federal money may be used for: food inspectors, education, student loans, job training, space exploration, scientific research, national parks, highways and railroads, prisons, cleaning up air and water pollution, and building and maintaining federal office buildings. These activities take nine cents of every budget dollar.

LAW ENFORCEMENT AND GENERAL GOVERNMENT (2 percent)

Paying the salaries of senators and representatives, their staffs, and other federal employees, the Secret Service, and Federal Bureau of Investigation (FBI), and other national law enforcement agencies, takes about two cents of every dollar.

SOCIAL SECURITY (34 percent)

Anyone who is employed is aware that something more than withheld (prepaid) income tax is taken out of their paycheck. For millions of workers, the Social Security tax, also called the Federal Insurance Contribution Act (FICA), they pay will be higher than their income tax at the end of the year. Some people pay no income tax, but everybody pays the Social Security tax.

Social Security is a government pension—money paid each month to retired and disabled workers. Germany was the first country to enact old-age pension laws, in the 1880s. The United States adopted it in 1935. It has since been expanded to include **Medicare**—health insurance for people collecting Social Security payments who have reached the age of 65. More than 45 million Americans receive Social Security payments each month.

Social Security may be the furthest thing from your mind today, but it has become a bigger issue that the income tax, and may affect your future taxes even more. The debate over what to do about fixing the system may still be going on by the time you are able to vote and begin your own career. It's not too early for you to begin to understand how these tax issues will affect your life.

The problem is one of numbers. When Social Security began over 65 years ago, there were fewer older people than there are today. People didn't live as long in those days. There were many more working people than the elderly. Gradually, over the years since then, the number of older people—those over 65—grew at a faster rate than the working members of the population. So the workers had to pay higher taxes to provide the money for the retired people.

Today, thanks to improved health care and new drugs, people live longer. The over-65 group is growing faster than the rest of the population. There used to be five workers paying the Social Security tax to support each retired person.

FEDERAL INCOME

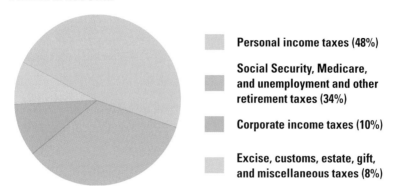

- Personal income taxes (48%)
- Social Security, Medicare, and unemployment and other retirement taxes (34%)
- Corporate income taxes (10%)
- Excise, customs, estate, gift, and miscellaneous taxes (8%)

FEDERAL EXPENSES

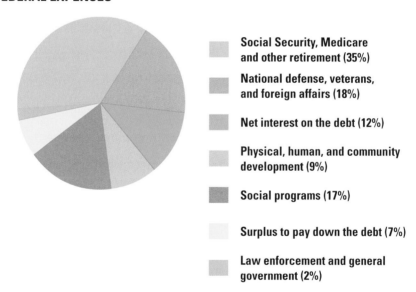

- Social Security, Medicare and other retirement (35%)
- National defense, veterans, and foreign affairs (18%)
- Net interest on the debt (12%)
- Physical, human, and community development (9%)
- Social programs (17%)
- Surplus to pay down the debt (7%)
- Law enforcement and general government (2%)

Now there are only three workers. And, since people live longer, they receive more payments during their lifetime. By the time you begin holding a regular job, there may be even more people collecting Social Security than there are today. Soaring medical and prescription costs also strain the Medicare system, which is partly paid for out of everybody's paychecks.

The big question is: where will all the money come from? That will concern you, because you will be one of the people paying the taxes. One possible answer is higher taxes. Another is to raise the age at which people can begin to receive the pension payments.

Another suggestion is to do away with the cap or limit on how much of a person's income is taxable. Unlike the income tax, which is called a **progressive tax**—the more you earn, the higher tax rate you pay—the Social Security tax is a **regressive tax,** the opposite of a progressive tax: the more you earn, the lower the tax rate you pay. As of 2000, the amount of income subject to the Social Security tax was limited to $76,200. Someone who earned $76,200 paid the same amount of tax as the person who made twice as much, or 10 times as much, or 100 times as much.

Another idea for fixing or reforming Social Security is to allow working people to invest some of the money they now pay in taxes so that it might grow in value. This would give them more money to draw from when they retire. Those who like this idea say that individuals can invest their money better than the government does. Those who disagree say that the **stock market** is too risky, that people might take out the money and spend it before they retire, and there is no way to guarantee that the money will be there when it's needed. Some people suggest that the government take part of the Social Security taxes they collect and invest it in the stock market.

Americans save very little of what they earn. Their use of **credit cards** and the amount they owe keeps going up. Both of these habits work against a more secure retirement system.

Like all tax questions, Social Security reform was a hotly debated political issue in 2001. Two United States senators,

John Breaux of Louisiana and Judd Gregg of New Hampshire, wrote:

> "But the truth is everyone agrees that the current Social Security system is unsustainable and that changes must be made to be sure money is there to support the baby boomers [people who are now 45 to 55 years old, and will begin to qualify for Social Security payments about the time you begin working] and beyond.
>
> "While the debate rages as to whether personal [investment] accounts should be above or within Social Security, most understand that personal accounts are a vital tool for all Americans to create wealth."

For purposes of the federal budget, both income from this tax, and Medicare and retirement expenses are included. But they just about equal each other, the taxes accounting for about 34 percent of total revenue, and the payments equaling about the same piece of the expenses pie.

Law enforcement agencies exist at every level of government: the FBI, state troopers, county sheriffs, and town policemen.

State and Local Taxes

In addition to the federal government, states, counties, cities, and towns rely on a variety of taxes to raise the money to provide services for their residents. People may vote on whether to create or increase a tax to pay for a specific project. Sometimes these tax increases win in an election; sometimes they are defeated.

Take a look around your school. Where did the money come from to build it, to buy the books and paper, pay the teachers and principal and secretaries, the cooks in the cafeteria and the custodians? School buses, the fuel they use, and the drivers—all this takes money.

Let's begin with the school itself. Like building a house, the money to put up a new school is usually borrowed. The school board may decide to borrow the money by selling bonds, notes that will have to pay interest and be repaid one day, like a mortgage. But the taxpayers in the county may have the right to vote on whether to do this. If they vote not to borrow the money, the new school won't be built.

Most of the money used to operate the school system comes from property taxes. (The federal government also funds many school expenses.) The property tax is based on the value of all the property in the county or school district: houses, apartment buildings, stores, factories, office buildings, even empty lots. It does not include churches and government buildings or parks. Each piece of property is assessed by a tax **assessor.** The amount of tax owed by each property owner is based on that estimate. In some parts of the country the voters have passed laws limiting the property tax rates, or how much they can be increased each year.

Taxpayers have rights. If someone believes that their property has been assessed at too high a value, they can

State Income Tax

All but nine states have an income tax that is paid in addition to the federal income tax. All but five have a sales tax, ranging from four to seven percent.

The states that have no income tax are: Alaska, Florida, Nevada, New Hampshire, South Dakota, Tennessee, Texas, Washington, and Wyoming.

The states with no sales tax are: Alaska, Delaware, New Hampshire, Montana, and Oregon.

Fighting fires is one of the vital public services that cities and towns must provide. Nobody objects to paying taxes for this kind of protection.

appeal to an appeals board and present their case. In 2001 the former governor of Maryland, William Donald Schaefer, objected to an increase in the assessed value of two town-houses he owned. He said they had been labeled as having a water view, which would increase their value. Schaefer said that he would have to stand on the roof to see a nearby river and creek.

The question the voters are asked to vote on sometimes involves an increase in the sales tax. A sales tax is a tax charged on almost anything you buy. It generally does not apply to food you buy in places like a supermarket, or to prescription drugs. If you buy food already cooked, like a burger and fries, you'll pay the tax on that. Suppose your state has a five percent sales tax. If you buy a toy or a battery or a pen for a dollar, you'll be charged another five cents for the tax. When you buy a pair of shoes for $40, you'll pay $2 more for the tax. Sales taxes may also be charged on services, such as video rentals and dry cleaning. It doesn't matter how much or how little you're spending, the tax rate is the same for everything.

The schools are the biggest expense for most counties or other school districts, taking half the budget. But states, counties, and cities have to provide many other services as well. Public safety is a big item in many government budgets: state police, sheriff's departments, and city or town police forces, their salaries, cars, and other equipment. The courts—judges, bailiffs, security people—are public employees. Jails and prisons are part of the public safety system.

Every time you hear a fire engine's siren, it means that firemen are responding to a call for help. Firemen do a dangerous, necessary job. They are paid to do that job. They have to be trained. Even in small towns that depend on volunteer fire departments, the fire engines and other equipment comes out of the public safety budget.

The roads and highways you travel on cost money to build and maintain. The interstate highway system has been built by the federal government. State highways are the state's responsibility. But the local streets where you live and go to school are the responsibility of local government. Whenever you see a crew out digging up a street or repaving one, or painting the lines down the middle of the highway, you are seeing tax dollars at work.

There are lots of things we take for granted in our daily lives. We don't stop to think that someone had to plan it, supervise it, and do the work that's involved. For example, everything you throw away seems to disappear. Where does it go after you put it in a trash can? Every city and town depends on people to pick up the garbage and take it away to a dump or landfill or incinerator. In some places this is a private business. In others, it is a public service. In either case, the people who want the service have to pay for it.

You probably never think about where the water comes from when you turn it on in your home to wash your hands or get a drink. But somebody had to build and maintain a system to make the water safe to drink and get it to your house. Sometimes this is a private company. But often water is supplied by a municipal (city or town) system.

In municipal budgets, many of these items are lumped together under the heading "public works." Public safety and public works are usually the two biggest slices of the expenses pie.

Governments don't do anything to earn income. They don't produce any products or sell anything. They are not operated like businesses, trying to make a profit. States can and sometimes do take in more money than they spend in a year. That gives them a surplus—like a profit—for the year. Unlike the federal government, states are generally prevented by law from operating at a deficit (a loss). They are not allowed to spend more than they collect in revenues.

The main source of revenue for these cities and states is the people who live there and the tourists who visit. (Sometimes they get money from the federal government, but that money comes from taxpayers, too).

"There is no free lunch," is an old political fact of life. It means that if people demand better roads, new schools, pay raises for teachers or police, more parks—whatever they ask from any level of government, somebody has to pay for it. About half the revenue collected by a city or county usually comes from the property taxes. In some counties, an income tax and a share of the state sales tax are important sources of revenue.

State income taxes are similar to the federal income tax discussed in Chapter Three. The tax forms are simpler and the tax rates lower than the federal ones. Cities and counties may tack on their own income taxes. Some states have begun to tax the income an athlete earns while playing in that state, even if they don't live there. A player on the New York Yankees, for example, would have to pay a California income tax on that part of his salary he earned while the Yankees were playing in Oakland or Anaheim. This is the kind of situation that usually ends up in a court of law.

Most states rely heavily on the income tax and sales tax. Although you see the sales tax added to the cost of things you buy, it usually amounts to just a few cents. So you don't think of it as paying taxes. It doesn't have the impact of an income tax that is taken out of a paycheck or paid all at once. But over time it can add up.

There are some taxes that are not as visible as the sales and income and property taxes. Some are called fees. The prices you see posted at gas stations include state taxes ranging from 5 cents a gallon to 26 cents, on top of federal gas taxes. Areas that draw a lot of tourists often put high taxes on the things that nonresidents are more likely to pay for, such as rental cars and hotel rooms. Taxes of some kind, regardless of whether they are called taxes, take a nip out of just about everything people pay for. Many of them are not noticed: a few dollars added to a telephone bill; a few more on an airline ticket.

Some of these taxes are called fees. Anyone who has to take out a license to open a business is paying a form of tax. The cost of automobile license plates, drivers' licenses, and car inspections are a kind of tax.

More tax money is used to operate the public schools than any other expense in most counties. The money comes primarily from local property taxes and state taxes.

The taxes on alcohol and cigarettes are examples of taxes used to discourage people from buying a product. State taxes on cigarettes vary from five cents to $1.00 a pack. The states where a lot of tobacco is grown or processed generally have the lower taxes.

Just about anything that has to do with living—and dying—has tax consequences. States have taxes on property that people leave to others when they die. National estate taxes may be eliminated in the next decade.

In 2001 the Tax Foundation estimated that the average worker had to work form January 1 to May 3 just to pay all the taxes that would be collected by local, state, and federal governments. That means that all the income the person

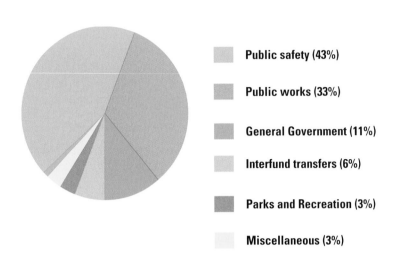

- Public safety (43%)
- Public works (33%)
- General Government (11%)
- Interfund transfers (6%)
- Parks and Recreation (3%)
- Miscellaneous (3%)
- Economic Development (1%)

Small towns and big cities tend to have similar sources of income and kinds of expenses.

earned, about one-third of all their income for the year, went to pay taxes of some kind. The rest of the annual income was what the person could spend. This is an average, because taxes vary widely among states and cities. For example, the lowest total tax bite among states was in Alaska, the highest in Connecticut. In most states the total tax bill takes about 33 percent of a family's annual income. Among cities the range was wider. The estimated state and local taxes for a family of four averaged $1,769 in Jacksonville, Florida, and over $6,000 in Philadelphia, Pennsylvania, and Portland, Maine. Tax considerations are one factor in some people's decisions on where to live. In addition to its warm climate, Florida attracts many older people and retirees because it has no income tax or inheritance tax. That's one reason some people prefer to live and die there. Some athletes and entertainers choose Nevada as their residence because it has no state income tax.

Taxes, as Ben Franklin observed, are as certain a part of life as death. Disagreements about what should be taxed, how much the taxes should be, and how the money should be spent by governments, are equally certain to continue throughout your lifetime. But, as President Franklin D. Roosevelt said in 1926, "Taxes, after all, are the dues that we pay for the privileges of membership in an organized society."

Assessor—one who determines the rate or amount of tax owed

Budget—a spending plan that lists income and expenses

Credit card—a plastic card enabling the holder to buy something with borrowed money then pay it back at a later date

Deductions—money spent on such things as medical expenses or interest on a home mortgage that may be subtracted from income before calculating the amount of tax a person owes

Deficit—an excess of expenditure over revenue

Democrats—members of the Democrat political party, which stands for broad social reform and favors an enhanced governmental role in social and economic life

Duty—a tax that a government collects on foreign products that are brought into its territory; also called a tariff

Estate tax—a tax on the property left by a person when they die; also called an inheritance tax

Excise tax—a tax on the manufacture or sale of goods; a business license

Exemptions—a source or amount of income not subject to taxation

Exports—goods that are sold outside of their country of manufacture

Faculty tax—a tax based on occupation, not income

Flat tax—a tax of uniform rate that does not vary depending on income

Imports—foreign goods that are brought into another country for sale

Income tax—a tax based on the amount of income earned during a year

Interest—a fee paid for the use of someone else's money

Internal Revenue Service (IRS)—United States government agency that administers the tax laws and collects taxes

Medicare—a federal health insurance program for citizens age 65 and older

Progressive tax—a tax plan in which higher amounts of income or purchases are taxed at higher rates; also called a graduated income tax

Publican—a resident of the Roman Empire who paid for the rights to collect the taxes

Regressive tax—a tax plan in which higher amounts of income or purchases are taxed at the same or lower rates than lower amounts

Republicans—members of the Republican political party, which favors a restricted governmental role in social and economic life

Revenue—another term for income

Revenuers—government agents in charge of collecting taxes

Sales tax—a tax paid on a purchase

Smuggling—the illegal importation of goods into a country

Social Security—a government-sponsored pension system that pays a monthly income to retired or disabled people

Stock market—a place where orders to buy and sell stocks are brought together and filled by brokers acting as agents for the public

Surplus—an amount left over after needs and use are satisfied

Tariff—a tax on imported goods paid by the importer

Tax—a fee charged by a government to raise money for its use

Carson, Gerald. *The Golden Egg: The Personal Income Tax.* Boston: Houghton Mifflin, 1977.

Gordon, John Steele. *Hamilton's Blessing: The Extraordinary Life and Times of Our National Debt.* New York: Walker & Company, 1997.

Griswold, Wesley S. *The Night the Revolution Began.* Brattleboro Vermont: The Stephen Green Press, 1972.

Kramer, Samuel Noah. *History Begins at Sumer.* Philadelphia: University of Pennsylvania Press, 1994.

Shaviro, Daniel. *Making Sense of Social Security Reform.* Chicago: University of Chicago Press, 2000.

page

2: Associated Press/Wide World Photos
6: Associated Press/Wide World Photos
9: Associated Press/Wide World Photos
12: Associated Press/Wide World Photos
16: Associated Press/Wide World Photos
19: Associated Press/Wide World Photos
20: Associated Press/Wide World Photos
22: Associated Press/Wide World Photos
25: Associated Press/Wide World Photos
28: Library of Congress

32: Associated Press/Wide World Photos
36: Associated Press/Wide World Photos
38: Associated Press/Wide World Photos
43: Associated Press/Wide World Photos
47: United States Government
50: Associated Press/Wide World Photos
53: Associated Press/Wide World Photos
57: Associated Press/Wide World Photos
58: Town of Easton Maryland

NORMAN L. MACHT is the author of more than 30 books, many of them biographies for Chelsea House Publishers. He is the president of Choptank Syndicate, Inc., and lives in Easton, Maryland.